Yaya's Cloth

Yaya's Cloth

Poems

Andrea Potos

Iris Press
Oak Ridge, Tennessee

Iris Press is an imprint of the Iris Publishing Group, Inc.

www.irisbooks.com

Library of Congress Cataloging-in-Publication Data

Potos, Andrea, 1959-
Yaya's cloth / Andrea Potos.
    p. cm.
ISBN 978-0-916078-65-2 (hardcover : alk. paper)
ISBN 978-0-916078-66-9 (pbk. : alk. paper)
I. Title.
PS3616.O845Y39 2007
811'.6—dc22

2007004002

ACKNOWLEDGMENTS

Artword Quarterly: "Making You Live in this Way"

Atlanta Review: "Greek Courtyards," "Talking About Scents with My Cousin"

Blue Fifth Review (online): "Persephone in the Field"

Calyx: A Journal of Art and Literature by Women: "Christmas Eve," "Yaya's Sweets," "Kerchiefs"

Claiming the Spirit Within: A Sourcebook of Women's Poetry (Beacon Press): "To My Still-Unconceived Daughter"

Diner: "Gossip"

Essential Love (Grayson Books): "Newborn Night"

Iris: "Mother/Daughter Dresses"

Kalliope: "After His Massage"

The MacGuffin: "Origins"

Montserrat Review: "At the Exhibition," "Persephone Remembers Hades," "Demeter Has a Premonition"

Nimrod: "In the Beginning, the Lens"

North American Review: "Each Self"

Not What I Expected (Paycock Press): "The Calling"

Paterson Literary Review: "Against Despair"

Poem: "Crocheting in Autumn," "Self-Doubts"

Poetry East: "Morning Ritual"

Poets On: Loss: "The Egg"

Prairie Schooner: "Crocheting the Shawl," "Sculptress"

River Oak Review: "The Word *Heart*"

Rosebud: "My Aunt Tells Me How it Was When She Was a Girl"

Silverfish Review: "How the Writing Changes"

So To Speak: A Feminist Journal of Language and Art: "Transitions," "Childbirth in the Dream"

Southern Poetry Review: "Greek Easter"

Standing on the Ceiling (Foxfold Press): "New Mother in September"

The Texas Observer: "Papouli's Hands"

Urban Spaghetti: "Leaving the Body," "Pregnant Woman at the Market"

Wisconsin Academy Review: "To Begin a Poem"

Wisconsin Poets' Calendar: "Pregnant Woman at the Market,"
   "Root"
Wisconsin Review: "The World Upside Down"

Several of these poems first appeared in the chapbook, *The Perfect Day*, published by Parallel Press of the UW-Madison.

My abiding gratitude to my father, who first taught me to love words and books.

Many thanks to Joan, Lori, Mary F., Bobbie and Stephanie, who always believed my book would find its way into the world; and to precious Lexi and to Michael, who make poetry possible.

To the Kosmopoulos women:

Penny and Alice,
and in deepest, loving remembrance of
Betty (1940-2006)
and Aristea (Yaya) (1908-1997).

CONTENTS

III.   WHERE GRIEF THRIVES

IV.   TRANSITIONS

CODA

In the Heart

The driftless area
is where I want to reside—
land the glaciers did not
grind down, flatten
with the force of deep ice,
leaving only broken
rocks in their wake.
There is the sweeping
dance of valley and hill,
the greatest beauty where loss
has been left to the elements,
sculpting its own natural shape.

I. Origins

ORIGINS

"Yaya" is Greek for grandmother

Yaya unwraps the cup
I gave her, its handle molded
into an angel.
She claps her hands like a happy child,
traces the glistening
arcs of its wings
and holds it to her cheek.
Eenay poli ohreho she cries,
the original words
I cannot translate alone—
they spill through her speech

more and more now,
as if she is letting slip
that knot of English,
leaving the dock where she arrived
seventy years ago   streaming back
to that girl in Piraeus,
port of her childhood
where I cannot go,
blue water of her birth.

From the Old Country

My grandmother Yaya calls to tell me
she was once a girl—
she remembers everything she says:
she has seen the worms spin their silk
in a town called Kalamata;
she has gone with her mother to the factory
to bargain over the price of such gold.
When they fed the silkworms mulberry leaves,
the room filled with the crunch
of greedy mouths—she laughs—
real silk it was she says,
I will tell you more.

     It is then I want to rush the ninety miles to her house,
sit on her brocaded couch, listen to the lustrous
weaving of her years—
I want to hear everything—
up until now, thinking my life began with me.

LITTLE MISS MUSTACHE

I'd plucked the beasts from their roots,
or so I thought, not expecting the trail
of prickly black weeds to grow back,
rebel stubble I'd have to keep yanking
no matter what, I could not escape
the nickname the 8th grade boys
stuck on me.

Legs I could reasonably shave,
arms I could hide with long sleeves, but that
shadowy stretch haunting my upper lip, oh
it needed an onslaught—
99 cent drugstore creme left me red
and raw, smooth and free
for one day.

My Greek relatives would say:
All that hair is in your genes.

BEFORE

Every day, in the refurbished café,
I am stopped by the gold-edged photo
of the city before my birth—
the now-vanished tracks
engraved deep in that ground,
elm trees lining both sides of the road,
branches like sunlit swords tipped to honor
those passing under.

The trolley will round the corner
to carry my grandmother in her brown silk
Saturday hat, netting swooped like tiny birds
across her face. She is younger than I am,
a bride from the old country,
she holds my eight-year-old mother's hand.
My mother's almond eyes are sheened with delight—
more and more English rises slowly through her Greek.

They will ride the nine miles downtown,
to the Riverside Theatre—
Katharine Hepburn in *Little Women*
on the bright marquee—
it will be my favorite story fifty or more
years from here, but for now, no one
has even dreamed of me. The picture
is that complete.

MARY

She reigned in my grandmother's house—
over the kitchen sink,
above the carved headboard of her bed,
on her glass-planed dresser, she was circled
by a coil of light.

Though in Sunday School
we heard about her son
who saved the world,
God the father, with his
invisible, potent seed,
it was the virgin, mother, wife
who lived in our dailiness
while we helped our grandmother scrub,
drain and dry each dish, every meal
like a repeating prayer;
while we brushed out our curls,
parted our hair on the side, with barrettes;
and while we napped
on the sprawl of white chenille spread,
waking up under Her watch,
patterns of vines and roses
pressed into our skin.

KERCHIEFS

*Greek women tied kerchiefs around their heads
in the ancient sign of modesty to hide their hair,
woman's glory.*
— Helen Papanikolas

I am not here to boast myself,
to steal my husband's mind from his tasks.

I milk the family goats,
hang the wash on bushes to dry.
I gather twigs for winter's fire,
mold the holy bread with my hands.

I keep my beauty furled
until moon time
when my husband snores, my children
lie sprawled in their dreams.

Then, I unknot this tie,
let my dark wings loose to the night.

On Mother's Day, Six Roses

For Yaya ("grandmother" in Greek)

When my mother and I enter your living room,
you lead me to the picture
my aunts framed for you,
a girl in Greece—you stand
with your brothers Kosta
and Paul, sisters Dina and JoAnn,
your black hair sweeping
like satin folds past your waist,
the dark sheen of your dress.
Your lips are stern, unsmiling—
as if you knew
you'd be the one left,
the one to store their losses
like worry beads carried
in a pouch of your heart.

This Mother's Day, your nephew
has sent you six roses
from the bush Dina planted thirty years before.
While you and my mother talk,
I stare at the petals,
stroke their silken heads bowing
over the rim of the glass—
purple nebulas on deep yellow, pink arcs
radiating crimson and indigo
like a watercolor painting, like the sky
just as the first stars
burn through dusk.

GREEK COURTYARDS

I read how Kazantzakis traces water and salt—
his urges to gather any spilled grains,
to shut off the tap
before water needlessly spills,
how he names this his father's
desert father—the Bedouin—
embedded still in his blood,
and I wonder at the way
I cannot bear any walls,
how I rush outdoors
at the first warm breath of day,
as in the open courtyards

where lives were made
among scent of acacia, oleander;
my grandmother's mother
rinsing linens in wide tubs,
drawing cool water from the well,
laying down the grapes to dry;
with my grandmother, small Aristea, beside her,
Aegean breeze ruffling her skirts,
her kerchiefed hair,
as she embroiders a trail of roses
and birds on sun-dried cloth.

Finding My Grandmother on a Greek Island

I followed the aroma up the narrow
street of Apollonia, twin village to Artemonas,
up toward the whitewashed walls of a house,
one of so many with the blue shutters
and doors, blue like a being itself.
Through the open door— an ivory cloth
with hand-done tatting trailed
along the edges of a dining room table,
a bowl of red eggs in the center (eggs
dyed for Christ's blood). I moved
a few steps; the kitchen's casement window
angled out where I stood near—held by the sound
of someone humming and chopping, perhaps onions,
beans or leeks to include in Easter supper,
a *kapama* sauce simmering from someplace
in the past behind her, everything
set in motion for the family to arrive.

GREEK EASTER

Somehow it always came after
that other, so-called Easter, a week or even
a month later, the cries and shouts of *Christos anesti*
around my grandmother's table mysteriously
lengthened for the occasion
and crowded with platters of succulent lamb
and *macaronada*, the golden rings of her bread
with blood-red eggs
planted in the dough, sesame seeds
encrusted around them,

while my sister and I and our girl cousins waited
in our eyelet-best, silk roses or lilies pinned
to our shoulders. We wore lace-rimmed anklets,
white patent leathers unearthed from shoestore boxes,
their surfaces so unscarred we could find hints
of our own reflections there, or maybe invisible Jesus
who knew the true, right time to return.

CHRISTMAS EVE

"It seems that in each life
a moment comes that the heart adheres to..."
— Connie Wanek

My grandmother's long drapes parted to reveal
her miniature tree strewn with gold
globes and white lights—my beacon
as I dodged the ice and rushed up to the sound of her
hands clapping as she ushered us all
into her apartment (so warm it could have been tropical);
and my ancient grandfather wobbling towards us, laughing;

all evening the chatter of my mother and sister,
cousins and uncles and aunts,
tinkling of ice and soda in tall glasses,
before my grandmother unveiled
the crystal platter crowded with her amber *baklava*,
her snowy *kourambeides*, and the ones I craved
all year—*melamakarona*—her magic
mingling of moist and dry, cinnamon and honey
seeping onto my tongue as she fed me
another and another. I knew then
how impossible it was
that she would ever die.

GOSSIP

She enjoyed it as much as cooking or eating.
It was an important part of living.
—Marie Giordano

Didn't the grandmothers convene
at their kitchen tables, fingers patting

floral oilcloths as they sipped
their percolated coffee swirling

with crumbs of toast and cake,
as they spoke

of what could not be contained:
the news, like love, that must be shared,

the hunger and loneliness at the root
quelled,

the confirming replies:
Ah, ah.

Syruping the Melamakarona

I come home to you
to begin what my Greek grandmother first taught me.
Measuring one part cool water
to two parts sugar, I pour it all
in the pot so shining it shows my face.
Over an arc of even flame, I stir
with the scarred wooden spoon I have dug
from the drawer. I wait
thinking of you waiting for me
to return wholly, heart
undivided.
I stir in slow circles, until the cloudy mass
burns into clarity—a liquid
richer than water
that will sweeten the amber cookies I'll dip
till they hold the gradations
of moist and dry, like days
of richness and drought.

GREENS

I want to be like those women
my mother knew as a girl in the '40s—
my Yaya and the other Greek ladies
who boarded the city bus on Saturday
summer afternoons, rode west
to the Menomonie River Parkway
where they scoured the sloping lawns,
the long, green banks along the water
with cloth bags slung over their arms.
They parted lush growth ticking
with invisible insects to find the vines,
the wild grape leaves they rolled
into *dolmades* that same night
or stuffed into jars on their pantry shelves.
They plucked dandelion greens
from the dirt—what most people never dreamed of
they scrubbed, steamed and tossed
with a little oregano, salt and olive oil
into a tender succulence. They knew where the raw
unpicked possibility thrived.

My Grandfather's Back

My aunt tells me she remembers
the sunscorched width of it,
iridescent strips of skin peeling
like the frayed wings of dragonflies.
She was twelve that summer day
he laid the flagstones
under the backyard trellis swing
that would be my sister's and mine—
flying under the shady clusters
of dusty, purple grapes and leaping onto those stones,
a path my grandfather
bent to the earth to plant, fitting
uneven edge to edge, making a runway
where we would one day land.

My Father Hates Garlic

He won't enter my house if I've used it
within the last week.
He says he smells its stench under the skin.
I plead for its medicinal powers;
he says he'd rather get sick.
I argue: how can a pure Greek like yourself...
but he shooes me away.

So I imagine the young boy
on the Eastside streets of Milwaukee.
That boy with skin the sheen of olives,
hair that shone like obsidian.
How different he must have looked
beside the bland American boys at school,
boys with their lunchboxes packed
with tuna casserole, ham or bologna sandwiches on white;

how they must have huddled together, watching
the strange-skinned boy eating
his buttery feta-cheese pie, his spicy oregano meatballs,
how they must have whispered: *Greasy Greek,*
Garlic Eater.

MORNING RITUAL

Even when the coffee is no good,
smells like the stained sides
of an old metal pot,
when cream doesn't ease
the taste, nor a gasp of cinnamon stirred
into its turbid depths, even then you drink it because
it is the pith of autumn outside
and the coffee is brazenly hot,
alive. The wrap of your fingers around
the porcelain mug nearly humming
from its well of heat
feels like a gesture from long ago,

some necessity
steeped in your blood,
perhaps from your grandmother,
that woman who loved you
with a heart scoured by loss.
You were a child, swinging your legs
off the red vinyl chair of her kitchen,
tracing the curve of roses on her oilcloth,
eating her toasted bread
as she sipped and nodded
and formed your morning,
patting your hands with her
nearly-translucent skin.

WEARING THE SILK

I am wearing the memory
of mulberry leaves my great-grandmother kept
in her pantry cupboards in Greece
(leaves she hand-picked each week),
my grandmother's glee when as a child
she roamed sleepless one night through
the house in Kalamata. Eighty years later,
she tells me she heard
the worms munching their leaves
where they lived under a cake cover on the shelves,
beside bins of sugar and semolina,
jars of olive oil and anise seed,
the gentle insistence of their task
as if swallowing moonlight to carry
through my grandmother
down to me, this whisper
of solace, draping of balm on my bare arms.

PAPOULI'S HANDS

(Papouli is the Greek word for "grandfather")

His house in Roumeli is rubble now.
Aunt Betty returned with stones—
I keep one, small monument
on my nightstand—streams of white quartz
pressed, glittering in grey rock.

In the nursing home—the vinyl chair,
metal-framed bed piled thick with blankets—
I go to him.
He is tapping his fingertips together—
a silent rhythm
I have watched all my life.

At 102, he says there are *so many things
not to think about.*
I imagine breadlines, his savings
lost, his son dead at three years old,
all that was never said.

I clasp his hands; they are always cool,
as if heat must rise from too
great a distance. His skin is smooth
as candlewax, thin as parchment
or the membranes of wings.
I trace their raised lacery of deep
purple lines, like the veins of an ancient country
I want to know.

AFTER JUNE 21

I imagine the darkness
sneaking up from
behind us, light
receding like an ancient promise
or the voice of my late grandmother
over the backyard fence at dusk,
unpinning the laundry from the lines,
folding and patting
into her blue basket
the sun-rinsed shirts and sheets,
seersucker playclothes and terrycloth towels
we pressed to our bodies,
laid down and dreamed upon in our beds.

II. Yaya's Cloth

Yaya's Mandolin

Memory strums faintly through my mother.
She was two, and there was constant
music for one month
in the three-room apartment over the diner.
A mandolin on loan for Yaya;
her own left for her brother Paul
when she sailed forever from Greece.

When asthma killed him,
there were no sons left.
Great-grandmother passed on the mandolin
to a village boy.
I did not know what you wanted,
she cried to Yaya.
Yaya shakes her head when she tells me,
and I wonder what happens
to all the words, the music
never released—
if they are locked, like loss,
inside the heart's silent house,
so that a woman must play her mandolin
without stopping—
even while her daughter sleeps—
the mother who knows truly
her joys are not hers to keep,
but are borrowed
and must be returned to the world.

PENNY & TOMMY

In memory of Tommy Kosmopoulos (1935-1939)

In the picture you show me, Mother,
of the two of you behind your father's restaurant,
the breeze blows back
the long white collar of your dress as your hand
cups the small knoll of your brother's shoulder,
your other hand a perch for his plump one,
his bellbottom pants like tiny sails billowing with wind
as he squints into sun and smiles
as if summer will be long
and generous this year.

You haven't yet sat down with your book
on that wooden bench under the dappled June light,
an arithmetic problem on your mind
when he wandered in the garage to retrieve his tricycle—
you haven't yet heard his scream
ripping open the air,
the fire of his scream
scorching a path through our history—

      where was the angel
    to scoop him up in her wings
  just before he fell into that pot of boiling broth
the cook set out to cool, the shadow of her wings
    sweeping across the pages of your book as she flew off
        to leave you free?
    Where was the voice that hovers in your ear:
Follow him in there Penny
    Follow him in

To My Twin Aunts

When I think of your mother,
I know now
how she is the bravest of all women, witness
to her boy dying of burns that June night, holding her vigil
by the iron bed that cradled his small body,
watching those doctors and nurses
who could not soothe his pain.
They put hot compresses on him—she said,
they would never do that today.
      And she dared again, her womb
enlarged and enfleshed itself for the seeds
of another child, for the bonus
of two of you this time,
she went ahead and did it,
pulled you both out into light, saying *yes* again, *yes*
to this life
that could not save him.

WINGS

When I was tall enough to peer over the edge
of her mahogany dresser, I saw it there—the gold filigree frame
with the picture of my mother at nine, holding the hand
of an auburn-haired boy wearing shiny white-laced shoes,
their cheeks doused pink
from the photographer's blush, behind them
a thicket of trees so green it was black.
Yaya told me how
my mother once had a brother, and she, a son,
before my aunts were born: *Tommy*, she would say,
my boy.

      And I thought about Tommy who would have lived
if God had not snatched him up
the one instant they turned away—my flesh and blood
who might have given me airplane rides with his arms,
twirling me around Yaya's lawn while I shrieked
at family picnics with his wife and their kids.
We could have all chased dragonflies together—
my favorite sport then—we could have caught them
between our fingertips,
trapped them inside Yaya's clean pickle jars
seeing the bluegreen fire of their wings
flutter wildly against the glass graves
whose lids we could open just in time, just in time
to watch them fly free.

As Stars

For my mother

Five days after her brother's funeral,
she returned to her classmates,
who offered graham crackers and cupcakes
from their lunchpails, a copy of *Bambi*.
They returned to their lessons, the ones
about the solar system, their home
planet the Earth, traveling huge circles
around the sun which was really a star,
though it appeared a blazing yellow,
not the far-away-blue of stars,
and even in orbit, the earth was turning
on its axis—a spin
so fast
it seemed still. Scientists said
it was in perpetual motion, but she knew they were wrong,
she could look around and see everything
fixed in its place—
her mother's tombed expression, the hollow
where her father had once been.
It must be a made-up story,
like the one they'd told her
after Tommy died, *It wasn't your fault*, they'd said,
but she felt the truth
branded into her body
as his was branded by the hot water
when she looked away—the truth
permanent, still,
forever as stars.

Yaya's Cloth, 1940

Yaya moves through the chores of her days
in the mornings out in the yard
her arms, a basket brimming with damp linens—
faded sheets, towels, tablecloths embroidered
and once washed by her mother's hands, by her own hands
since she was a girl of ten
when her brother died and her mother told her:
It's time for you to learn what a woman must do.
        It is the summer after her own son's death
and she hears those words
as she spreads the linens out wide over the line,
taking clothespins from her bulging apron pocket, sheets
flapping against her bare arms
as she pushes the wooden pins into place, smoothing
the creases to be ironed again
by the wind, the sun.
And she stops now, brushing her cheeks against the cotton
streaming
    as if the rinsed cloth still holds the smell of his skin
as she breathes in the threadbare
cloth of this survival.

My Aunt Tells Me How It Was
When She Was a Girl

She would discover my grandmother
at the kitchen sink, weeping
for her son, dead at three years old,
the brother my aunt did not know,
only snatches of words overheard:
Tommy my boy, oh
that one afternoon.

My grandmother insisted the water
run nearly scalding over her bare hands,
the suds profuse and glistening
as each dish, cup
and saucer squeaked.
Against the porcelain,
her grief flowed clean.

AGAINST DESPAIR

My grandmother wept at her kitchen sink
for her son, dead at three years old;
through her long life, she crocheted 97 afghans,
sewed my dresses,
my mother's pillows and drapes,
cooked the succulent Greek chicken,
the *spanokopita* and *pastiscio*
for dozens at her Sunday table.

My grandfather in 1943
lost all his savings,
lay prone in his bed for weeks;
his youngest child would peek through the crack
in the door to see him, before
he rose to work sixteen hours
every day at his Harmony Diner

where my twin aunts scampered
behind the counter to build themselves
sundaes with extra cherries,
and my sixteen-year-old mother
sat upstairs in the office
becoming a grown-up,
typing the daily specials:
hot turkey with mashed potatoes and gravy,
grilled pork chops on a toasted bun,
layer cake a la mode, double malted milk,
and coffee, always coffee, five cents a cup
in those days, guaranteed strong
and hot, infinitely refillable.

The Egg

Mother, you say *There's nothing like losing a child,*
and you must know—
after your brother's death;
your mother moved through her days
as if underwater, and you
in her wake, gathered the egg she speared forth whole
oval, grey, smooth as newborn skin
from the womb of her loss—
the egg you carried
   and bore down through me,
a creature hunched inside there
with wet wings like silk knotted
and tangled as it pushes
against the hard caul
to find its way free.
   I want to tap the thick shell, break it—
I want to see the cracks
spreading
like the map of the earth on its surface.

48

Heaven

At 86, tears wet your eyes as you say
you *never expected to live this long,*
that your baby brother, your baby son
still wait for you there.
Then you tell me what you always
remember—a girl of seven
in Kalamata, mornings you awoke
to the sound of rinsed linen flapping on the line.
Your window opened
wide to the vast white light, air of orange
and lemon blossom, opalescence of sky
and sea, blue tourmaline water in the distance,
and fig trees circling
the whitewashed walls of your house.
I like to think of you here—
before you knew grief—the sister
who will go with her brothers to gather
mulberry leaves for the worms her mother keeps
in the pantry cupboards, so in the dark sleep
of their cocoons, they may spin
a miracle of silk.

GRANDMOTHER'S TABLE

The word spreads slowly,
like warm honey
on my tongue—*grand mother*, rising
through memory's bounty.
Does my mother see
how I stand up straighter when I speak it—
grand mother—as if recalling an empress
or Demeter herself.

Her son had been dead twenty years
when I was born into her life.
From the apartment above her, I travelled
alone through the winding
tunnel of stairs to her door—
her kitchen, opening
like a fan of light
where her table was ready.
She filled bowls with Greek soup, fed me
cookies curved like the moon,
bread sliced warm off the loaf, toasted
and dripping gold
on the plate. She let me pour the milk
in her coffee and watch the rising of white,
like thunderclouds in her cup.

When I was born into her life,
her heart was nearly emptied
of its clotted sorrow, rage,
all the unused love
she couldn't offer my mother as a girl—
it rushed like grain from an open sack
down to me.

YAYA'S SWEETS

Yaya, you say every morning you wait for sun
to light the blue dome of the Greek church
outside your window.
You prepare your table—cups and saucers,
spoons on handstitched linen,
for your friends in the apartments downstairs,
women you've known longer
than your husband or your three daughters.
They will gather in your kitchen,
bedrock under your days, these women
who brought the sweets to your house,
sat with you for hours
after your son Tommy
died, fifty years ago this year;
sweets you learned as a girl
in Athens with your mother,
and what you have shown me to make—
baklava steeped in honeyed syrup then sliced
into diamonds; *kourambeides,* like buttered crescent moons
powdered with sugar;
and *koulouria,* touched with anise and best
for dunking. Winter afternoons in your kitchen,
the ivory walls burnished by low blonde light,
I'd wear your apron strewn with pale cabbage roses,
the cotton soft as the flour
I poured in the bowl
when you'd tell me it was time,
the air dusting white around us
while you turned and mixed the dough
with your bare hands,
what we would shape and braid
into wreaths, circles, figure eights.

Curtains In Spring

In memoriam

Finally, the windows raised, rinsed air billowing
sheer curtains behind me, resonant air I breathed
on my grandmother's street, 52nd Street in the '60s,
Aunt Betty with the cat-eyed glasses parking her Plymouth
at the curb, Liddle Kiddle dolls on the sidewalk,
my freshly chalked hopscotch tower, grandmother's
trowel and spade, evergreens rising to the wooden railing
of her porch, her living room window, bevelled glass shining
reflecting ocher drapes trembling with a breeze from
the other world the curtain lifting   for a moment believing
she is near.

THE KINDNESS OF STRANGERS

Swarthy and dishelleved, clutching a sheaf of mail,
he followed me up the walk
to my Yaya's apartment: our center
for Greek feasting before she died, the dining room table
with the extra leaf in the middle, the kitchen
where she passed on the truths
of *tiropita* and *pastiscio, melamakarona* and *kefthedes*
while in the living room, my husband and Papouli
chatted and drank the occasional highball.

I'd urged my husband to pull up to the curb
so I might peer through the glass: the long, lit hallway,
floral green carpet, the burnished bannister
that had ushered me into her warm rooms.
This man, this stranger behind me,
reached the door as I did.
Was I looking for someone? *Kosmopoulos,*
I told him. *Yes,* he said, *my mother lives upstairs,
my mother will remember her,*
smiling as he cradled the door, like the door to time,
the slimmest pathway through hope, memory ajar
in his hands, for those moments
I slipped through.

CROCHETING THE SHAWL

Because I don't know the finishing stitch
for this shawl, I end up at the chain bookstore
under florescent lights, ploughing through
Crocheter's Companion, Easy to Make Crochet.
What I want is my grandmother
sitting beside me on her Duncan Fyfe sofa.
I want her alive, calling me
Koukla, her needleworked pillows
nested on the cushions,
in air infused with the scents from the open doorway
of her kitchen—olive oil, cinnamon,
oregano, the promise
of abundance.
I need to see her hands once more, age-spotted
and nimble, the fluid motion of her fingers
as natural as singing
or breathing, her voice telling me
how I can
complete this piece without her.

TRAGEDY

From the old country,
I pinned an evil eye
under my baby's mattress—
black orb in an aqua sea
guarding her
in sleep's oblivion.

From the old stories
I learned you must always set a place
for the thirteenth fairy,
a place-card etched in your blood.
Don't for a moment
let her feel brushed-off.

Happiness is a frail and tender soul,
a sickly child destined
not to live too long.
It is the other—that fierce hulk of a force
with all the stamina—stalking you through the ages,
eternally waiting
for that moment you forget.

III.   WHERE GRIEF THRIVES

The Origin of Children

In Sunday School they won't tell you
how, after God rent water,
plants and all those creatures
from the firmament,
on the seventh day when he
was too weary to finish the task,

the Grandmothers arrived, bearing all
in their great hands.
On the fold between
ground and sky
they knelt,
passing the children down,
naming each child
one by one
creating
the world each time.

With this Hurt

She gathers the bent twigs, burnt
gold leaves fallen
in her grandmother's backyard.
She builds a nest
in the hollow
around her heart:
the crushed silver wrappers of her childhood,
strands of her sister's long hair,
even the black nubs
shaved off her father's face.
She falls asleep to the sound
of small birds breaking
open their mouths.

SCULPTRESS

In that indigo space before sleep
she remembers hard
her dead grandmother's face—
long hair wound back and up,
eyes deeply engraved,
thick forest of lashes;
she hears even her grandmother's voice
calling inside the rough stone
as she closes her eyes,
chips away at this immense
block of loss bequeathed to her,
releasing the beloved form.

THREE OLD FRIENDS

We collect hurts like bright dead butterflies
pinned to our bulletin boards.
We unwrap them like old candy
mummified in lint from our pockets.

For every wrong they come up with,
I can match with one better.

Like playing jumprope at recess,
one of us
is always in the middle.
Another waits for her turn, the moment
the skipping one trips and is out.

THE WORLD UPSIDE DOWN

The sisters would run from the house,
skip double-dutch rope,
build hopscotch empires
with pink and blue chalk.
With the neighbor kids they'd play red light green light,
catch me if you can, tag you and you're It.
They practiced backwards somersaults,
headstands on the front lawn, breathing in
the long damp grass that tickled their foreheads
as they studied the world upside down—
through the screen door,
their mother bent there over the kitchen sink, their father
circled by the evening newspaper.
Then, as dusklight dispersed
into the bonus of darkness,
fireflies sparked like wands at their fingertips
in these hours when they watched
their parents' lives—the father hiding
behind the television's hum, the mother
spiraling around him
like a moth seeking nectar
from the closed fist of the bud.

To the Coffee Shop

Praise to the early risers who unlock
the doors at 4 a.m., create
lemon blueberry crumble,
orange raisin scones dunked
headfirst in sugar,
oatmeal cookies stuffed
with cranberries and pecans.
Praise to the splash and sizzle
on the grill, smells rising
from childhood's deep cache,
when you entered the kitchen rubbing your eyes
and your father kissed you
over the top of his *Times,*
and your big sister looked ridiculous
with her milk mustache.
Your mother turned to greet you
as if you alone were the sun
while eggs burbled in her pan—
praise to the succulent yellow yolks
that were not yet broken.

THE WAY SNOW IN FEBRUARY

At the cemetery gates, the procession
drives off in relief to the restaurant.
Without appetite
for fish or bread, I stay behind, searching
for some trail through the ice-encrusted
snow that marks the path to his grave.

I find a green tarp, like a weak
disguise for emptiness,
flapping in the sharp wind.
I lift one edge, peer into
the sculpted hole in the earth,
this deep hollow
where they will lay my grandfather's body
when none of us are looking.

I want to return and reach
through the soles of my feet,
down into the hardened ground,
the way snow in February
sometimes melts its way through
the earth's waiting pores.

WHERE GRIEF THRIVES

Each morning a fresh ache bursts
into bud,
inside the walled garden where grief thrives.

I am searching for a way in—
through the tangle of brush that masks
the opening,
for some chink in the old brick,
or the rust-pocked key
that belonged to my grandmother.

I want to touch the bowed
blooms that must live there.
I want to cup my hands under
the fountain's water—a stream so steady
in its fall, it can carve out
a hollow in stone.

LEAVING THE BODY

Wind moans like the desert,
shatters windows, unhinges doors.
She evaporates
like the water she left boiling on the stove,
blue flame scorching the bottom of the pan.
She leaves with her laces flung loose,
her blouse undone till her breasts fly
like wailing children from her chest.

She forgets the groceries piled in their bags,
clothes crumpled down the chute,
all the dishes still to wash—her hands
that once moved through warm water,
brushing in perfect arcs over the rims of cups,
        reaching into the bellies of bowls,
the bone-sure ground of her life.

Root

You can't miss the strawberries
at the weekly farmer's market,
with their brazen red shining.
What turns your head today are the radishes
poised in a pyramid, the startling
dark pink of their skin,
as if some patient soul spent all night
clearing them of dirt, rubbing them
with the gentlest cloth till they shone;
as if someone saw beyond
their reputation as dusty,
tasteless root,
mere garnish
to what's real on our plate;
as if for once they were equal
with the great supermarket apple,
the garnets buried
in the pomegranate's blood.

AT THE EXHIBITION

An artist paints with his eyes, not with his hands.
—Renoir

I squeeze past men in wool blazers and hats,
mothers with babies yawning in their arms,
the teacher rounding up her class—
all crowded here for a glimpse
of the Master and his world.
On tiptoe I arch my neck for
Two Sisters On the Terrace,
son Jean with nursemaid Gabrielle,
good friend Monet
painting in his garden at Argenteuil.
In the last room, I watch the continuous
short film from 1915—Renoir
in his frail and withered body,
his gnarled and crippled hands.
Through the scratchy, hyper motion of the screen,
he is still at work—
the shutter of his gaze capturing
in an instant
what I cannot see—perhaps a table
laden with pears and apples,
roses trembling with life on the vines,
or the gates of the other world opening
like the light that flashes from his eyes and falls
on the blue meadows of his canvas.

In the Beginning, the Lens

During the first years of her career, Cameron used a lens that yielded an image where one plane would be in sharp focus, and the rest would blur… Her exposures would last as long as seven minutes.

—Julia Margaret Cameron, pioneer Victorian photographer, 1867.

In the beginning, the lens
knew more than I—
how to converge
on one pure facet of truth:

the eyes
weighted with sleep and obsidian,
the unstoppable cascade of hair,
the rose at the throat
of Ophelia.

I photographed Beatrice, Mary Mother,
the Angel at the Tomb who
could have been Magdalen;
the inner sorrow,
the rapture made real.

During the long interval of exposure,
my model might sigh, look beyond
the studio door. Her movement turned
to a blurred dream unfolding,
a breath caught—
proof of the Spirit in flight.

To Begin a Poem

You need only a scrap,
just one loose page
torn off the maps
that lead to treasure,

you need to hear the far-off cry—
echo of the child wandering
through the tangled woods,
waiting
for you to find a pattern
in the spill of crumbs
at your feet.
Come to her rescue
with a generous heart,
lean to her voice and listen
to her story:
this is how I came to be lost.

The Word *Heart*

The critique group warns me
I'm walking a tightrope when I use it.

Their mouths are flashing lights—their red pens
bars lowered at the railroad crossing.

We must all be watchful of this word.

It will stick like tar, drown a poem
in canned syrup
no one can stomach for long.

I look back on all the mistakes I have made—
even when I've tried excluding the word,
it's come back with a force
solely its own,
like the lover who won't give up,
like the muscle that must be used or die.

ON READING SYLVA PLATH

No frayed ends
or stray motion here,
only her words
like the petrified blood
of great pines,
ancient resins
of grief,

only her words
wrenched from stone,
tight as peat—
I smell the smoldering fires.

How the Writing Changes

The words start out small, tidy—
grids on a streetmap,
suburban houses where families
sit down to meat loaf and potatoes,
and the mother always serves herself last.
Then, as she rises to wipe the table,
she looks past her husband's mute face
to the clearing
through the kitchen window, the sky
burning to dusk and fireflies lifting
their lit bodies from the grass.
She opens the back door and heads for the stream
whose water she has heard in her sleep
for the flowing that leads to the river
where the white water rushes.

For My Friend Who Writes
of the Mediterranean

You give me salt,
the tourmaline sheen
of distant water,
olive trees trembling with dew,
stone, dust and heat,
the bones of grandmothers.

I lie under the fierce light
of your words,
a lost sun
drenching each pore.
A resonance of *Yes*
shines through me.

To Another Greek-american Writer

We have each sat ensconced
at our Yayas' tables;
sesame seeds, powdered sugar spilling
off plates and onto our laps.
We have heard the fathers' voices turn
opinions to facts in the dining room,
while in the kitchen our mothers and aunts
scrubbed the pots, passed along the news
not meant for the hearts of men.

After dinner we watched
in our grandmothers' hands
the yarn, the threads become
a hillside, a goat, a village girl
holding a bowl of just-picked olives,
or perhaps figs, pomegranates—those crimson jewels
of our underworld story
against a backdrop of ivory linen.

The Well

The surface is marred
with a scatter of last autumn's
forgotten leaves,
the limp remains of insects,
their drowned iridescence.

You must bend yourself slowly
to see over the edge,
let the long rope unravel
from the tight spool of your heart.
Like seams gently torn open,
let your hands part the dark water.

IV. TRANSITIONS

DEMETER HAS A PREMONITION

I grounded my daughter,
corralled her within
my own four walls.
She stomps her feet above me,
cries to her window's dreamy
blue beckoning.

I tried to tell her of
my bloodwarning,
but she cannot think beyond the girlmeadow
of her sure delight.
She sees the field where she plays
as seamless and green—
I see only the blackened
fingers of rupture
rising below
the blades.

Persephone in the Field

I never dreamed this field
contained anything but flowers,
that the ground had a mouth,
that a horned god
could loiter beneath roots
of tall grasses, weeds,
stalk me through the scope
of his greed,
with a hunter's stone patience
he could watch my movements—wait
for the angles of my imbalance
as I leaned to pick my mother's lilies.

PERSEPHONE REMEMBERS HADES

When he dragged me into the bowels
of his home, my eyes grew used to darkness.
When he crowned me with desire,
snarled and pushed his way in,
I believed him
when he named it *love*.

Every month, my blood
reminds me of pomegranate—
flesh split open in my palms, spill
of shining seed, juice staining my skin.

My mother says I'll get used to the light.
I don't tell her about the marks left
in my heart, the ache I possess
on certain days, how I squint
from the glare of my rescued life.

SELF-DOUBTS

They stick,
my socks pricked
with burrs, those barnacles
of the field; they suck at
the hem of my coat, my sleeves,
like some ravenous ex.
For days I feel their sting.

Worse, they turn to splinters
wedged
under the tender lip of skin.
The redness spreads,

I need
my beloved grandmother's needle
dipped in flame before it enters.

TO MY STILL-UNCONCEIVED DAUGHTER

My relatives ask me why
I am taking so long
to have you, they don't know
that each week I name you—*Aristea,
Helena, Penelope*—
all the mothers in my blood,
how I see you
in the nook of my arm,
your dark curls damp on my skin,
how I buy dolls and explain
they're for me—the African doll
with black braids, handpainted lips,
the rag doll with red yarn hair, fleecy green
pajamas, silk stitched mouth—
they are part of the widening circle
on my bed, with the honeyed bear, softer
than pillows, I tuck under my arm at night—
placeholders
until the day I recall you from reverie,
until I am large enough
to contain you, to bear love's pressure
on the walls of my heart.

While Pregnant

As if my belly were a divining rod,
I am drawn to find water.
Water leaks up through my words.

I want to lie beside lakes,
follow rivers to their source.
I want to wait on the ocean shore
while the tide reels up to encircle me
before tracing back
to its unfathomable beginning.

I want to submerge myself in poems
and the quiet of small waves lapping.
   One week before I knew,
I dreamed a creature—
a furled form
lowering deep in silver water
like an amniotic wash.

Nesting Instinct, 9th Month

Raising your belly out of bed with you,
you waken at 2 a.m. with an urge
to do still more while there's time.
You grab the dust rag off your nightstand,
move through the sleepy darkness softly
so as not to wake your husband, whom this impulse
does not strike.
Rag on your hand like a glove, you glide across
the shiny walnut finish of your grandmother's buffet,
the curves and hollows in the carved feet
of the dining room table she passed on to you.
You open drawers, lift loose tablecloths
and linens, you fold them
and match them edge to edge.

You move to the kitchen. The mess
behind the cupboards' glass doors is all you can see—
boxes of food long since expired,
pop tarts and powdered milk,
packets of oyster crackers snatched from cafe tables,
jars of chocolate syrup from those sundaes
you never made; you heap them onto
the growing trash, along with all those empty
containers you never filled with leftovers,
stacked for years—you don't need them
"just in case" anymore.
You wipe porcelain tiles with warm water,
pat them dry, the space around you cleared and glistening
as you smile at the wonder of not knowing
the exact moment you will be called
to lay down your cloth, come to your child
with your house, your life clutter-free.

CHILDBIRTH IN THE DREAM

I saw it coming, as if an earthquake
could be predicted
in the morning paper while I sat
and sipped my coffee from a porcelain mug.

I knew just when to stand ready
to catch my grandmother's china
as it tumbled off the shelves of the great
mahoghany hutch and shattered
on the groaning floor

as the chandelier swung like a rabid animal

I left my home
crossed over

before all the bridges collapsed

and the seas parted   and my body
announced the god.

NEW MOTHER IN SEPTEMBER

She remembers when she sank alone
into the grass sprinkled with fallen
leaves curled like the newly born, when she napped
warmed by early autumn.
This year she brings her child
to gaze with her
into a sunburst sky of maple and oak.
She cannot look for long, the child
is lifting fingernails of dirt to her mouth,
the child is dragging a twig
seriously close to her eye,
the mother must dart her eyes,
look and switch, scamper
back and forth between
her daughter and the sky,
stashing images
like a squirrel gathering nuts for the winter—
cache of simple beauty,
necessity of autumn fire.

Transitions

The woman in the umber dress told me
they are the *pregnant times*,
midrealms for pure
healing,

like those weeks before summer crowds us
with its somnolent green, its lush breath,

when the birds shout mantras of return,

before winter with its white hands
strokes every surface to silence,

when the leaves wrestle air—crimson,
gold, so holy with their death,

like those weeks after my daughter
emerged nicked and bloodied from
the tunnel of her birth,
when I paced and dragged through days
wondering when the ground
would rise to meet me,

when *mother* was a sound like sorrow
I had not yet swallowed
in my body that once grew her.

NEWBORN NIGHT

I rock while you suck,
your mouth bound to my breast
like some unbreakable seal.
My lids graze my eyes.
The clock ticks dumbly on.
Already beyond 2 a.m.,
and the whole world sleeps
without us. But then,
we drifted from them
long ago, dipping
and swelling in this sea of
exhaustion and need, and I
with no more memory of land
than you.

The Calling

My child's murmur breaks open
into a cry I can't ignore.
I lay pen and notebook down,
last images leaving like bright streamers
trailing behind me
from a party I must leave too soon.

Her cry keeps calling
like a mother's voice in the summer dusk
ordering her child in
from the generous lawns
where the child lingers—claiming
it can't yet be time to go in,
it's much too early for sleep—the fireflies
have only just appeared
leaping their messages of light.

My Daughter's Naps

were gleaming
coins I spent
each afternoon,

rich milk I swallowed.

They filled me.

Sated
with streams of generous silence,

I poured myself into her
lavishly   freely
when she woke.

MOTHER/DAUGHTER DRESSES

I couldn't resist them
in the spring Hanna Andersen catalog:
empire-waisted cotton as soft as new sand,
bright pink peonies splashed with green,
ample fabric grazing our feet.
My daughter clapped her hands
when I ripped open the plastic
that contained them; we twirled
briefly around the kitchen.

A friend told me to *watch your boundaries,*
as if there might be something blurred
and imprecise about me,
now that I've chosen
to be a larger version of my child
on certain summer days; petal mirroring
petal as we move, the flourish and boast of us together,
generous bloom before love
like the original cell she once was,
divides us.

TALKING ABOUT SCENTS WITH MY COUSIN

The autumn-warm smell of our grandmother's
avgolemono soup, simmering
on the back burner of our lives,
her pantry infused with sesame,
anise for Easter *koulouria*,
and now this, my non-religious cousin's
dose of the uncanny
one year after her divorce:
the aroma of church incense that followed
her throughout her day,
into her car, her office, the health club,
outside, inside, everywhere,
she could not locate the source,
remembering the censers swinging
from the priest's gnarled hands
in the church where our mothers
nestled in the close
communion of the Greeks,
the fathomless well of the cantor's voice,
the gold dome invisibly,
consolingly above us.

MAKING YOU LIVE IN THIS WAY

for my grandfather, on the fourth anniversary of his death.

This year, I don't light the chapel candle
I usually set before your photograph.

I quench my blaze of temper
when my daughter's will springs to block mine.

I kneel beside her
to cut out clouds from blue

and purple constuction paper.
I thank my husband for his morning impulse

of fresh bagels.
I hold his warm hands,

forget to look at the clock.
Calmness spreads like a meadow within me.

As the hours unfold, I repeat often
the one word you were known for:

beautiful, beautiful.

After His Massage

for my husband

On the way to the restaurant tonight,
he doesn't swear at poky drivers.
He navigates the lanes like rivers
ushering us where the lamps

whisper their glow. Across the table,
every piece of him sits with me,
a seamless body of light.
Words leave his mouth,
land on my chest
like nestling birds.

Our child is happily dreaming at home;
the sitter has all night to stay.
Between us right now, the old spasm
gives up and sighs.

Each Self

My six-year-old daughter stares into the purpling
copper sky and names it dusk, a just-learned word
she is happy to declare, comparing it to evening
and afternoon. We talk of how the earth turns away
from the sun each night,
a motion so encompassing,
our bodies cannot know it.
I don't tell her how the child
part of me still disbelieves it—that this globe
actually spins while we breathe, while my daughter
changes invisibly before my eyes,

her infant body submerged inside her
with her toddler waddle and her four-year-old skip,
each swallowed within the other
like the nesting dolls she keeps
on her new desk, each self
perfectly preserved, forsaken
for the one that must come after.

PREGNANT WOMAN AT THE MARKET

I spot her
ambling past mounds of parsnips,
the swelling tips of the first asparagus.
She is filling her cloth bag
with the deep blush of rhubarb.
Perhaps when she is home
she will make a pie, folding
and tucking dough over the tart,
diced fruit that will turn
miraculously sweet.

I want to linger here
in her radius,
shut my busy mouth so I might hear
the tiny hum of the world
becoming flesh.
I want to kneel on the dusty sidewalk,
rise when she passes,
the imprints of stones on my knees.

Deciding to Go to Greece for the First Time

It was in late August,
I watched my 8-year-old girl,
her ponytail stained with summer gold.
She turned to smile as she dipped her foot in the pool,
her whole slim body into the wavery blue.
With a long exhalation, I lay back, I let the word
float across me—*motherland*—I felt it
sink with the sun through my skin
down to the source,
my grandmother, my mother's mother Aristea,
who arrived from the Old Country, a bride of 19.
We lived in the flat above her, an easy journey
down the winding stairwell to her
open kitchen door,
simmering smells of lemon
and oregano, almond and anise seed.
Gone for these eight years, she glows
like a pilot light beneath the days.

GREEK LANGUAGE TAPES

I begin them as a chore:
te kanete, paro kalo, necessary
prelude to our upcoming journey,
thirty minutes in thirty days.
I am finding the sounds,
pieces of my grandmother's voice
flowing through my throat, syllables
that hovered in the air of her kitchen,
her den, when I was *Koukla*
eating her *dolmades, kourambeides,*
when my body heard
for me, stashing syllables
eenay—it is, *eemay*—I am.

Home from Greece

We've unearthed the trinkets and gifts,
cards of glittering blue-domed chapels
and whitewashed steps immaculate with sun,
silver strings of *komboloi*, worry beads
like those Yaya strung through her fingers,
those that lay on the mahoghany
table of my childhood.

We've made stacks of receipts for the scrapbook
(taverna bills, entry to the towering Acropolis),
collected the films to share with my mother and aunts—
Syntagma Square, Sina Street where we walked past the stone
building where my mother was born, infant daughter
brought to the New Country seventy years ago.

We've made lists of groceries we must buy,
though nothing like Yaya's Easter bread,
the red sauce for her *kapama*.
We're getting back to the business of the life
that waited for us here, awakening
long before we have ever woken—
beating the dawn to its task,
as if our bodies
have kept something of that light.

WHEN PEOPLE ASK ME WHAT IT WAS LIKE TO FINALLY BE IN GREECE

Should I admit my urges to kneel
on the Acropolis stones,
how I actually did
lay on the Hill of the Muses, cypress
and olive branches shading me
while I tried to absorb some oracular
song from the dirt;

instead what I heard was the daystruck
chatter of Greeks strolling the footpaths,
balm of their rapid and elaborate syllables,
my grandparents' conversations
at kitchen tables, Yaya's lifelong friends
Dina, Katerina; my mother, once a 7-year-old girl
who knew no English yet.

CODA

CROCHETING IN AUTUMN

I wanted the silence of yarn,
the hook, shining

movement of gold, in
and out, the skeins unravelling

at my touch.
I would be Penelope, undoing

her work each night, so as never
to reach the end of

this wool under my hands,
sprawled on my lap

and becoming
goldenrod, aster,

marigold, the plot of flowers
behind my grandmother's grave,

the sun that floods childhood
and all Septembers,

the maple leaves falling
where my grandmother lies.

ABOUT THE BOOK

This book is typeset in Sabon. A descendant of the types of Claude Garamond, Sabon was designed by Jan Tschichold in 1964 and jointly released by Stempel, Linotype, and Monotype foundries. The roman design is based on a Garamond specimen printed by Konrad F. Berner, who was married to the widow of another printer, Jacques Sabon. The italic design is based on types by Robert Granjon, a contemporary of Garamond's.

SECTION PHOTOGRAPHS

I—Aristea and George Kosmopoulos; Athens, Greece

II—Aristea (Yaya), Penny and Tommy

III—Papouli's house; Roumeli, Greece

IV—Acropolis, Athens; seen from the Hill of the Muses

FRONT COVER: cloth by Aristea Kosmopoulos

COVER PHOTOGRAPH: Jane Sutter

DESIGN: Robert B. Cumming, Jr.

—Michael Slater

ANDREA POTOS was born in Milwaukee, Wisconsin. She lived the first five years of her life in a duplex apartment above her Greek grandparents, and their spirit has remained an abiding presence and inspiration throughout her life and poetry.

Her poems appear widely in journals and anthologies, including the *Women's Review of Books, Poetry East, Southern Poetry Review, Prairie Schooner, Calyx: A Journal of Art & Literature by Women, Kalliope, Claiming the Spirit Within: A Sourcebook of Women's Poetry* (Beacon Press), *Mothers & Daughters: A Poetry Celebration* (Random House), *I Feel A Little Jumpy Around You* (Simon & Schuster) and *A Fierce Brightness: 25 Years of Women's Poetry* (Calyx Books).

She's received the James Hearst Poetry Prize from the *North American Review,* first prize in the poetry competition for *So to Speak: A Feminist Journal of Language and Art* and has been nominated for a Pushcart prize. Her previous collection of poetry is *The Perfect Day,* the debut collection in the chapbook series published by Parallel Press of University of Wisconsin-Madison.

She lives in Madison with her husband and daughter.

Printed in the United States
71138LV00002B/481-579